Cooking in the Nude

FOR BARBECUE BUFFS

Written by Debbie and Stephen Cornwell
Designed by Carolyn Weary Brandt
Edited by Dara Powers Parker

Library of Congress Control Number: 2002115723
ISBN 1-57427-135-0

Published by Howell Press, Inc., 1713-2D Allied Lane,
Charlottesville, VA 22903
Telephone: (434) 977-4006
http://www.howellpress.com

First Printing

HOWELL PRESS

TABLE OF CONTENTS

INTRODUCTION

Warning: When you play with fire…you may get *exactly* what you wanted! That is, a tender and deliciously luscious morsel, scrumptious and beautiful to behold, just begging for you to take that first bite…Whoa now, we are talking about dinner here, not your dining companion!

Whether your plan is to woo your sweetheart with a little candlelit dining *al fresco* on the patio; or on a beach blanket just steps from the surf, toes in the sand, watching the firelight sending sparks skyward; or on the rustic wood deck of a secluded hideaway with starlight twinkling and ice cubes tinkling in the glasses, romance is the evening's objective. *Carpe P.M.!*

Cooking in the Nude for Barbecue Buffs is here to inspire you and assure your success, even after the flames go out! Our succulent collection of mouthwatering recipes include specialties like "Saucy Aussie," "Bikini Fettucini," and "Chickalicious." We've included menu suggestions complete with wine recommendations to enhance your gourmet dining experience. So, fire up your grill!

All Barbecue Ingenues and grill masters agree about the importance of *Fun and Flames* (Barbecue Strategy and Charcoal Protocol). We'll show you how to make the most of a balmy summer evening when love is at *steak,* including tips on what to do with your aromatic wood chips and how to control your heat. You'll also learn how to be *Ready Grilling and Able* (Pantry Needs) and, when the right moment comes, to fan the flames of desire with a little *Firewater* (Libations).

Once you've worked your *Barbecue Voodoo* (Soups and Salads) you'll really be *Playing with Fire* (Entrees)! And if you time it right, you'll even have room on the grill for a little *Hotsee Totsee* (Side Dishes). Of course, how you end the evening is totally up to you. We'd recommend a little moonlight dancing, a sensual skinny dip, and your favorite "Amour du Jour!"

FUN AND FLAMES
(Barbecue Strategy and Charcoal Protocol)

*I*n order to be a flaming success, you have to have flames. To get flames, you have to choose a fuel and a method of igniting the fuel. If using a *gas* barbecue, open the lid, ignite the burners, then close the lid, and heat the grill for ten to fifteen minutes before cooking. If using a *charcoal* barbecue, you have several choices to ignite the charcoal briquettes. 1) Build a pyramid of charcoal on the grate, sprinkle with lighter fluid, and carefully ignite. 2) Use an electric fire starter by first piling charcoal on top; plug it in, wait ten minutes or until the coals are red, spread the coals in an even layer, and leave them to heat for fifteen minutes or until red coals are covered by gray ash. 3) Use a chimney starter by stuffing a crumpled up newspaper page into the bottom, set the chimney on the barbecue grate, fill with charcoal, and ignite the paper. After twenty minutes, or when red coals are covered by gray ash, carefully spread the coals evenly onto grate.

If you wish, you may throw aromatic wood chips or fresh herbs, such as sprigs of rosemary or thyme, onto the coals before placing the cooking grill on the barbecue. The wood chips will add a smoky flavor to the food; the herbs will add a lovely fragrant aroma that is guaranteed to whet the appetite of your dining companion.

Before you begin cooking, brush the clean grill lightly with oil to prevent the food from sticking. Slowly wave your hand about five inches above the grill. If you can hold it for one to two seconds, the fire is "hot," three to five seconds means the fire is "medium," and six to eight seconds indicates a "low" fire. After cooking, use a wire brush to clean the hot grill.

A few tips:

To control heat: 1) Adjust the height of the grill: higher for slower cooking, lower for faster cooking. 2) Push the coals apart for lower heat and slower cooking;

push the coals together for higher heat and faster cooking. 3) Open air vents for higher heat, or close air vents for lower heat.

To control flare-ups: Cover the grill and close the vents.

To prevent foods from cooking too fast: Once coals reach the gray-ash stage, spread them evenly around, leaving a little space around the edge of the grate. To slow your cooking down, move the foods to the outer edges of the grill.

To be the quintessential chef while projecting a cool but debonair command of the grill (and avoid having the evening go up in smoke), you must plan ahead. Avoid the marinade escapade. Prepare all sauces and marinades ahead of time, allowing the foods to develop their full, luscious flavors. With romance at *steak,* leave nothing to chance. Shop early for only the finest meats and the freshest seafood and produce. When you plan your table setting, display true savoir-fare and romantic flair with a vase of fresh tropical flowers or another equally extravagant centerpiece. Organize everything in advance. Arrange the utensils and ingredients on a nearby table. If it's compatible with your evening's menu, plan an appetizer that doesn't need to be barbecued to offer along with chilled glasses of your favorite libation. Set the night on fire with candlelight, not just at your table setting, but small votive candles scattered about the patio. Use the white twinkle lights left over from the holidays to add delicate mood lighting by draping a few strands on nearby trees and plants. Finally, sexy and exotic (did we mean erotic?) background music is a must, and, if you're a good dancer, be sure to save the tango CD for last. Remember that when your gourmet grilling is over, and the last coal is cooling, the night is your claim to flame!

READY, GRILLING AND ABLE

(Pantry Needs)

♥ ♥ ♥ ♥ ♥ ♥ ♥ ♥ ♥ ♥ ♥ ♥ ♥ ♥ ♥

apricot jam	farfallini or conchiglietti	pepper
artichoke hearts, marinated	garlic	peppercorns
	garlic powder	pine nuts
balsamic vinegar	garlic salt	polenta
basil	ginger	red peppers, roasted
bay leaves	Grand Marnier	red wine
beef broth	green curry paste	red wine vinegar
beer	honey	rice vinegar
black olives	horseradish	rosemary
black pepper	hot pepper sauce	sage
bourbon	jalapeños	salt
brown sugar	kalamata olives	savory
cannellini	lemon juice	sesame oil
capers	linguine	sherry
catsup	liquid smoke	soy sauce
cayenne	macadamia nuts	sugar
celery seed	maple syrup	sun-dried tomatoes in oil
chervil	mayonnaise, low-fat	
chicken broth	molasses	Tabasco
chili powder	mustard, coarse grain	tarragon
chipotle chilies	mustard, dry	thyme
cider vinegar	mustard, yellow	tomato paste
coconut milk, unsweetened	olive oil	tomato sauce
	onion salt	vegetable broth
cranberries, dried	orange marmalade	vegetable oil
croutons, herbed	oregano	walnuts
cumin	oyster sauce	white vinegar
Curaçao	paprika	white wine
curry powder	Parmesan, grated	wine vinegar
Dijon mustard	penne	Worcestershire sauce

FIREWATER
(Libations)

Whatever food is sizzling on the grill, grilling by its very nature and in any season is enhanced by an appropriate libation. On sultry hot days what could be cooler than an iced or blended frozen cocktail in a tall frosted glass? When you're out on the deck of your boat, a brilliant flower-covered patio, an utterly divine terrace, or stately southern veranda complete with ceiling fans, nothing satisfies more than a cold thirst-quenching concoction with a slice of lemon or lime. Please consider some of these classics.

Classic Margarita

2 oz. tequila
¾ oz. Triple Sec
1 oz. fresh lime juice

Combine all in shaker, add crushed ice, and shake until shaker is cold to touch. Rub lime wedge on rim of martini glass, dip in a saucer of salt, and pour in contents of shaker.

Frozen Daiquiri

1½ oz. rum
1 tsp. powdered sugar
juice of one lime

Combine all in shaker, add crushed ice, shake until shaker is cold to touch, and strain into frosted martini glass.

Tom Collins

2 oz. gin
1 tsp. powdered sugar
juice of ½ lemon

Combine all in shaker, add crushed ice, shake until shaker is cold to touch, and strain into tall frosted glass. Add several ice cubes, fill glass with carbonated water, stir, and add a toothpick with slices of lemon and orange and a maraschino cherry. Serve with a straw.

Planters Punch

juice of 1 lime
juice of ½ lemon
juice of ½ orange
1 tsp. pineapple juice
2 oz. light rum
1 oz. dark rum
2 dashes Triple Sec

Pour first 5 ingredients into tall glass filled with ice. Stir until glass is frosted. Add dark rum and top with Triple Sec. Add a toothpick with slices of lemon and orange and a maraschino cherry. Serve with a straw.

A Word on Wines

When choosing wines to complement grilled foods, have some fun. The smokiness and wide variety of marinades and sauces call out for flexibility and a sense of adventure. Lamb and Zinfandel are well-matched, big, rich flavors, but Sirah, Barbera, and Sangiovese also work well. Simple steaks long for full-bodied ripe reds like Merlot, Barbera, and Sangiovese; but intensified sauces and spices do better with Petite Sirah, Cabernet, and Zinfandel. Ribs are well matched to peppery Zinfandels or Shiraz, both of which also work well with good ol' hamburgers.

Chicken that is lightly seasoned pairs well with Sauvignon Blanc or even a light, fruity Riesling. The more you season your marinade or accompaniments, switch to Chardonnay or Viognier. And when glazed with sweet tomato-y sauces, think light reds like Chianti. Salmon, too, can be supplemented by a red wine—try a fruity Pinot Noir. If you're in a mood for white wine, Sauvignon Blanc or Chardonnay also work wonders with salmon, swordfish, or halibut. For a sweet snappy shrimp dish, try Pinot Grigio or Sauvignon Blanc.

Barbecued Pork Skewers

20 minutes
(marinate 2 hours)

Step One:

½ cup water
¼ cup soy sauce
2 Tbsp. sesame oil
2 Tbsp. rice vinegar
2 Tbsp. brown sugar
1 Tbsp. oyster sauce (optional)
¼ cup minced fresh cilantro
1" piece fresh ginger, thinly sliced

Whisk all ingredients in bowl until blended.

Step Two:

½ lb. pork tenderloin, 1" thick

Cut pork into thin strips, then cut strips into pieces about 2" long. Add to bowl and marinate 2 hours at room temperature, or longer in refrigerator. Thread pork onto skewers and grill over medium heat, turning often until done.

Artichoke and Red Pepper Spread

20 minutes

Step One:

3 oz. roasted red peppers, drained
    and chopped
3 oz. marinated artichoke hearts,
    drained and chopped
¼ cup minced fresh parsley
¼ cup freshly grated Parmesan
3 Tbsp. olive oil
2 Tbsp. capers, drained and rinsed
2 small garlic cloves, minced
½ Tbsp. fresh lemon juice

Combine all ingredients in food processor until finely chopped.

Step Two:

salt and pepper, to taste
parsley sprigs

Season mixture, spoon onto serving dish, and garnish with parsley. Serve with baguette or water crackers.

Avocados with Kiwi Mint Salsa

20 minutes

Step One:

½ Tbsp. honey
1 Tbsp. fresh lime juice
2 tsp. chopped jalapeño, seeds removed
4 mint leaves, chopped
1-2 kiwi(s), peeled and chopped

Combine all ingredients except kiwi in bowl and blend well. Then stir in kiwi.

Step Two:

½ avocado, peeled
mint sprigs

Thinly slice avocado and fan onto chilled plates. Top with kiwi salsa, garnish with mint, and serve.

Sun-dried Tomato Olive Toasts

15 minutes

Step One:

¼ cup butter, softened
2 Tbsp. freshly grated Parmesan
2 Tbsp. chopped sun-dried tomatoes
    packed in oil
2 Tbsp. chopped black olives

Combine all ingredients in small bowl.

Step Two:

1 baguette, sliced

Toast bread slices and arrange on serving plate. Spread with tomato butter and serve warm.

Mediterranean Salsa

20 minutes

Step One:

1 6½-oz. jar marinated artichoke hearts
3 Roma tomatoes, chopped
½ cup feta
¼ cup kalamata olives
2 Tbsp. finely chopped red onion
1 clove garlic, minced
2 Tbsp. chopped basil

Drain marinade from artichokes into a bowl. Chop artichokes and add to bowl. Add remaining ingredients and chill until ready to serve. Serve with crackers or baguette.

Charred Red Pepper & White Bean Soup

45 minutes

Step One:

2 red bell peppers

Halve, seed, and roast peppers over open flame or under broiler until charred. Transfer to paper bag, fold top tightly, and steam for 10 minutes. Scrape charred bits off peppers, chop, and set aside.

Step Two:

2 Tbsp. reserved oil from sun-dried tomatoes
1 Tbsp. minced garlic
1 tsp. savory
⅓ cup drained sun-dried tomatoes
3 cups vegetable broth
½ cup pasta, farfallini (bows) or conchiglietti (tiny shells)

Heat oil in frying pan over medium heat. Add garlic and savory, and sauté until garlic is tender. Chop tomatoes and add to pan. Blend broth into pan, increase heat, and bring to a boil. Add pasta and boil 5 minutes.

Step Three:

1 15-oz. can cannellini (white kidney beans)
salt and pepper, to taste

Reduce heat to medium. Rinse and drain cannellini, then stir into soup. Stir roasted peppers into soup. Continue cooking until pasta is just tender, or al dente. Season with salt and pepper.

Mixed Greens with Honey Tarragon Vinaigrette

20 minutes

Step One:

3 Tbsp. light olive oil
1 Tbsp. honey
1 Tbsp. red wine vinegar
1 clove garlic
1 tsp. dried tarragon
½ tsp. Dijon mustard
salt and pepper, to taste

Combine all ingredients in blender and mix until thick. Adjust seasonings.

Step Two:

mixed salad greens (e.g., red leaf, romaine, butter, frisee, endive, spinach)
herbed salad croutons

Tear greens into bite-size pieces. In large bowl, toss greens and croutons to mix. Add a little dressing and toss to coat. Serve on chilled plates.

Grilled Corn Salad

30 minutes

(marinate 45 minutes)

Step One:

2 ears corn on cob, shucked
vegetable oil

Brush corn with oil. Grill over low-medium heat, about 15 minutes, until lightly browned, turning often. When cool to touch, cut kernels from cob.

Step Two:

⅓ cup chopped fresh cilantro
2 Tbsp. lime juice
1 Tbsp. lemon juice
2 tsp. olive oil
2 tsp. sugar
½ tsp. salt
¼ tsp. pepper
⅛ tsp. garlic salt
1 cucumber, peeled, seeded, and chopped
1 firm ripe tomato, chopped

Combine all ingredients except cucumber and tomato in bowl, stirring until blended. Stir in cucumber, tomato, and corn until well coated. Cover and refrigerate until chilled, about 45 minutes. Stir again before serving.

Grilled Tomato Basil Salad

Step One:

2 firm ripe tomatoes, quartered
salt and pepper, to taste

Sprinkle tomatoes with salt and pepper. Grill over medium heat, until lightly browned on all sides, about 8-10 minutes. Tomatoes should hold shape, but soften slightly.

Step Two:

1 Tbsp. olive oil
1 Tbsp. lemon juice
1 clove garlic, mashed
¼ tsp. Worcestershire sauce
½ cup chopped fresh basil
salt and pepper, to taste

Whisk all ingredients together until blended. Gently turn tomatoes in dressing, cover, and marinate 20 minutes. (If you prefer a chilled salad, marinate in refrigerator.) Just before serving, remove garlic. Optional: toss large seasoned croutons in with tomatoes before serving.

♥ Born To Grill

I'm a thrill a minute, but let's take our time!

1 hour, 30 minutes

(marinate 1 hour)

Smoky Sweet and Spicy Tri-Tip Roast

Step One:

½ cup brown sugar
¼ cup paprika
1 Tbsp. black pepper
1 Tbsp. chili powder
¾ Tbsp. garlic powder
1 Tbsp. onion salt
¼ tsp. cayenne
2-3 lb. tri-tip roast
oil, as needed

For spice rub, mix first seven ingredients together in jar. Rinse roast with water and pat dry with paper towels. Lightly rub roast with oil, then massage spice rub into roast, using 1-2 tablespoons per pound. Cover loosely and marinate 1 hour at room temperature.

Step Two:

¼ cup oil
½ onion, finely chopped
⅓ cup finely chopped green pepper
1 clove garlic, minced
1 cup catsup
¼ cup dark brown sugar, firmly packed
¼ cup molasses
2 Tbsp. Worcestershire sauce
2 Tbsp. yellow mustard
2 Tbsp. fresh lemon juice
1 Tbsp. cider vinegar
1 tsp. hot pepper sauce
½ tsp. liquid smoke

For barbecue sauce, heat oil in large saucepan over medium heat. Sauté onion, pepper, and garlic until soft. Add remaining ingredients and continue to cook 25-30 minutes, stirring frequently. Remove from heat and let cool 1 hour to let flavors blend.

Step Three:

Brush roast with barbecue sauce and put on oiled grill over medium heat. For medium rare, cook 10-12 minutes per side with lid closed. Reposition as needed and baste occasionally with sauce. When done to your liking, remove roast from heat, cover with foil, and let rest 10 minutes so juices stay in meat.

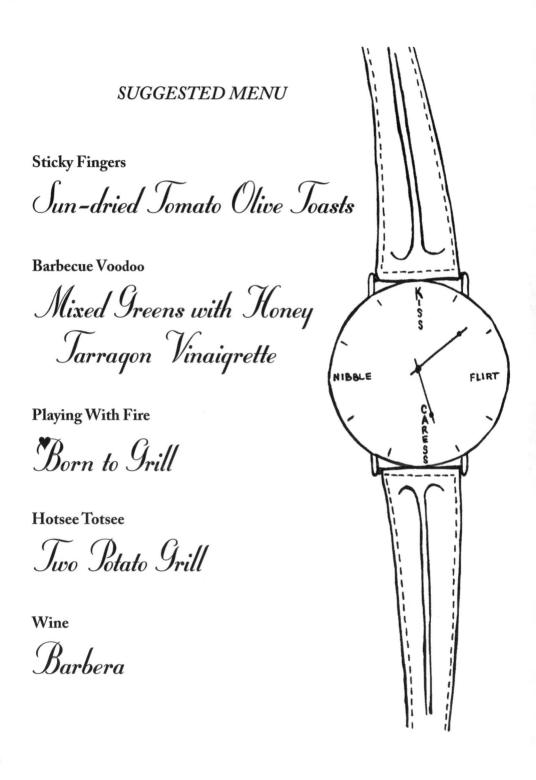

SUGGESTED MENU

Sticky Fingers

Sun-dried Tomato Olive Toasts

Barbecue Voodoo

Mixed Greens with Honey Tarragon Vinaigrette

Playing With Fire

Born to Grill

Hotsee Totsee

Two Potato Grill

Wine

Barbera

True Confessions

I can't rib without your love!

Succulent Beef Ribs

Step One:

1 red bell peppers

Halve, seed, and roast pepper over open flame or under broiler until charred. Transfer to paper bag, fold top tightly, and steam for 10 minutes. Scrape charred bits off pepper, chop finely, and put into 2-quart saucepan.

Step Two:

1½ cups catsup
½ cup honey
¼ cup brown sugar
¼ cup Worcestershire sauce
¼ cup water
1 small onion, finely chopped
1 Tbsp. Tabasco
1 Tbsp. cider vinegar
1 tsp. garlic powder

Combine all ingredients in 2-quart saucepan and blend well. Bring to a boil, reduce heat, and simmer until onion is tender.

Step Three:

3-4 lbs. ribs

Cut beef ribs apart. Tenderize by boiling or pressure-cooking prior to grilling. If using pressure cooker, add ribs and 1 cup water or beer to cooker, bring to full steam, turn back to gentle rocking motion, and cook 10 minutes. Cool under running water until pressure is released. If boiling, add ribs to pot, cover with water, and boil 1 hour.

Step Four:

Marinate ribs in sauce for 1 hour. Grill over medium heat for 20-30 minutes, turning and basting frequently with sauce, until evenly browned.

SUGGESTED MENU

Sticky Fingers

Artichoke and Red Pepper Spread

Barbecue Voodoo

Grilled Corn Salad

Playing With Fire

True Confessions

Hotsee Totsee

Grilled Polenta with Herbs

Wine

Petite Sirah

♥ Love Machine

Test your love power!

Curried Beef Kabobs

Step One:

1 Tbsp. chipotle chilies
1 clove garlic, peeled
1 Tbsp. curry powder
½ Tbsp. olive oil
1 cup plain yogurt
1 small red onion, minced

Combine all ingredients in blender and blend until smooth. Transfer to medium bowl.

Step Two:

1 lb. beef fillet or sirloin, cubed

Put beef in bowl and toss to coat. Cover and set aside at room temperature, 1-2 hours.

Step Three:

Thread beef cubes onto skewers. Put skewers on oiled grill, turning to brown evenly on all sides. Allow 7-8 minutes for medium rare, or until done to your liking. Remove to heated platter and serve.

TEST YOUR LOVE POWER

● Cutie Pie

Sexy ●

● Flirt

Hottie ●

● Oooh Baby!

Red Hot Lover ●

SUGGESTED MENU

Sticky Fingers

Avocados with Kiwi Mint Salsa

Barbecue Voodoo

Charred Red Pepper & White Bean Soup

Playing With Fire

♥*Love Machine*

Hotsee Totsee

Grilled Ratatouille

Wine

Zinfandel

Hunka Hunka Burnin' Love

Let's make sparks fly!

Bourbon Beef Kabobs

Step One:

½ cup brown sugar
½ cup chopped fresh cilantro
⅓ cup soy sauce
⅓ cup bourbon
¼ cup fresh lemon juice
2 tsp. Worcestershire sauce
1 cup water
1 tsp. dried thyme

Whisk all ingredients together in small bowl, until well blended.

Step Two:

1 lb. beef fillet or sirloin
oil, as needed

Trim fat from beef and cut into 1" cubes. Put beef in dish, pour marinade over, cover, and refrigerate 8 hours, stirring occasionally.

Step Three:

parsley sprigs

Thread beef onto skewers. Grill kabobs over high heat, turning often. Cook 7-8 minutes for medium-rare, or longer as desired. Remove to serving platter or plates and garnish with parsley.

SUGGESTED MENU

Sticky Fingers

Mediterranean Salsa

Barbecue Voodoo

Grilled Tomato Basil Salad

Playing With Fire

Hunka Hunka Burnin' Love

Hotsee Totsee

Mediterranean Vegetables with Olive Pepper Relish

Wine

Cabernet Sauvignon

Rated "R" For Romance

This evening is intended for lovers only and may contain playful flirting, tender kisses, and unbridled passion.

Beef Fillet with Rich Mushroom Tomato Sauce

Step One:

1 cup sliced brown mushrooms
2 Tbsp. minced shallots
1 Tbsp. butter
½ cup beef broth
¼ cup red wine (e.g., Cabernet, Merlot)
8 sun-dried tomatoes, packed in oil
½ cup sour cream
2 Tbsp. bourbon
1½ Tbsp. chopped fresh parsley
fresh ground pepper, to taste

In large frying pan, cook mushrooms and shallots in butter over low heat until soft. Add broth and wine, and boil until liquid is reduced by half. Place tomatoes on paper towels, pat dry, chop, and add to sauce. Add remaining ingredients and simmer, stirring often, until thickened, about 15 minutes.

Step Two:

2 beef tenderloin steaks, 1" thick
parsley sprigs

Grill steaks on oiled grill over medium heat, turning every 2 minutes. Cook about 4-5 minutes for rare, 5-6 for medium. Remove to heated plates, nap with sauce, and garnish with parsley.

SUGGESTED MENU

Sticky Fingers

Artichoke and Red Pepper Spread

Barbecue Voodoo

Grilled Tomato Basil Salad

Playing With Fire

Rated "R" for Romance

Hotsee Totsee

Grilled Asparagus

Wine

Cabernet Sauvignon

Amour du Jour

Let's cook up something special tonight, oooh la la!

Veal Chops in Mustard Peppercorn Sauce

Step One:

⅓ cup dry mustard
¼ cup sherry
¼ cup Dijon mustard
¼ cup coarse grained mustard

For mustard sauce, put dry mustard in bowl and gradually whisk in sherry to make a paste. Whisk in mustards. Can be stored in a sealed container in refrigerator up to 2 months. Use in salad dressings and sauces.

Step Two:

1½ Tbsp mustard sauce
2½ Tbsp. olive oil
1½ Tbsp. soy sauce
1½ Tbsp. sherry
1 Tbsp. rice wine vinegar
1 green onion, minced
1 clove garlic, minced
1 Tbsp. minced ginger
½ tsp. peppercorns, drained and mashed
½ tsp. pepper

For marinade, whisk mustard sauce, oil, soy sauce, and sherry until blended. Blend in remaining ingredients.

Step Three:

1 lb. veal chops, 1" thick

Using meat fork, tenderize chops by poking all over both sides. Put chops in shallow dish and rub marinade into chops. Cover and marinate for 4 hours at room temperature, or refrigerate overnight.

Step Four:

Remove meat and bring to room temperature. Grill over medium heat on oiled grill, 4-6 minutes per side, rotating to create crisscross grill marks. Remove to heated platter, cover, and let rest 5 minutes.

SUGGESTED MENU

Sticky Fingers

Sun-dried Tomato Olive Toasts

Barbecue Voodoo

Charred Red Pepper & White Bean Soup

Playing With Fire

Amour du Jour

Hotsee Totsee

Grilled Ratatouille

Wine

Merlot

Haute Buns

…are très chic!

20 minutes

(marinate 2 hours)

Steak Sandwich with Caramelized Onions

Step One:

2 Tbsp. soy sauce
4 Tbsp. balsamic vinegar
2 sirloin or tenderloin steaks, ½" thick

Whisk soy sauce and vinegar together in small bowl. Lay steaks in dish, pour marinade over steaks, and refrigerate for 2 hours.

Step Two:

1 Tbsp. butter
1 Tbsp. olive oil
1 large onion, thinly sliced
1½ tsp. sugar

In large frying pan over low heat, melt butter and oil. Add onions, sprinkle with sugar, and cook slowly, 15-20 minutes, until rich golden brown. Remove pan from heat, cover, and keep warm.

Step Three:

½ lb. brown mushrooms
sourdough buns
parsley sprigs

Meanwhile, thread mushrooms on skewers and brush with marinade. Put mushrooms and steaks on oiled grill over medium-high heat. Cook steaks for 3-6 minutes per side. Grill mushrooms until tender. Just before removing steaks, add buns, cut side down, toasting until done. Place open bun on plate, top with steaks, then mushrooms, then onions. Garnish with parsley.

SUGGESTED MENU

Sticky Fingers

Artichoke and Red Pepper Spread

Barbecue Voodoo

Grilled Tomato Basil Salad

Playing With Fire

Haute Buns

Hotsee Totsee

Two Potato Grill

Wine

Cabernet Sauvignon

The Grill of My Dreams

...is a Bar-be-cutie!

Chicken on Spinach with Grilled Peppers

Step One:

3 Tbsp. olive oil

1 Tbsp. balsamic vinegar

1 red bell pepper, quartered lengthwise and seeded

1 yellow bell pepper, quartered lengthwise and seeded

1 onion, sliced ¼" thick

6 large mushrooms, sliced ¼" thick

Mix oil and vinegar in small bowl. Brush vegetables with mixture and grill over medium heat until quite tender, turning often. Remove to bowl. Cover and keep warm.

Step Two:

2 boneless, skinless chicken breasts

Brush chicken breasts with vinegar mixture. Grill over medium heat, turning 2-3 times and brushing with mixture, until chicken is opaque throughout and juices run clear when pierced with fork, about 15-20 minutes.

Step Three:

1 Tbsp. olive oil

1 clove garlic, mashed

1 lb. spinach, washed and stems removed

¼ cup pine nuts

1-2 Tbsp. white wine

1-2 Tbsp. freshly grated Parmesan

While grilling chicken, put oil in frying pan and cook garlic over low-medium heat, 1-2 minutes. Add spinach and nuts to pan, and sauté over medium heat until spinach is limp. Add wine as needed for moisture. Divide spinach onto center of warm plates and top with peppers. Lay chicken on vegetables and sprinkle with Parmesan.

SUGGESTED MENU

Sticky Fingers

Sun-dried Tomato Olive Toasts

Barbecue Voodoo

*Charred Red Pepper &
White Bean Soup*

Playing With Fire

The Grill of My Dreams

Hotsee Totsee

Grilled Polenta with Herbs

Wine

Sauvignon Blanc

# Fan Dance

Fan the flames of desire and you may start a bonfire!

Spicy Citrus Chicken

Step One:

1 can frozen orange juice, thawed
1 cup canned tomato sauce
¼ cup honey
3 Tbsp. fresh lemon juice
3 Tbsp. fresh lime juice
1 tsp. minced orange zest
1 tsp. minced lemon zest
1 tsp. minced lime zest
4 cloves garlic, crushed
1 tsp. salt
1 tsp. dried thyme
³/₄ tsp. cayenne

Combine all ingredients in large bowl and mix thoroughly.

Step Two:

2 chicken breasts, skinned

Add chicken to bowl, turn to coat, cover, and marinate 4 hours, or longer in refrigerator. Remove chicken to platter. Pour marinade into saucepan and boil 1 minute.

Step Three:

lemon slices

Place chicken on oiled grill over medium heat. Grill, turning 2-3 times and brushing often with marinade, until chicken is opaque throughout and juices run clear when pierced with fork, about 20 minutes. Transfer to warm plates, garnish with a twist of lemon, and serve.

SUGGESTED MENU

Sticky Fingers

Avocados with Kiwi Mint Salsa

Barbecue Voodoo

Grilled Corn Salad

Playing With Fire

Fan Dance

Hotsee Totsee

Two Potato Grill

Wine

Vioqnier

French Kisses

Let's say "Oui!" to joie de vie and get carried away tonight!

Grand Marnier Glazed Chicken

Step One:

¼ cup Grand Marnier, or other
    orange liqueur
½ cup apricot jam
¼ cup white vinegar
1 Tbsp. Worcestershire sauce
1 Tbsp. Dijon mustard
1 Tbsp. honey
pinch cayenne

Combine all ingredients in small saucepan over medium heat and simmer, stirring often, until well blended. Cool to room temperature.

Step Two:

2 chicken breasts, skinned

Put chicken breasts in shallow dish, pour marinade over, and turn to coat. Cover and refrigerate 4 hours or longer.

Step Three:

mandarin orange slices
2 Tbsp. minced fresh parsley

Place chicken on oiled grill over medium heat. Grill, turning 2-3 times and brushing with sauce, until chicken is opaque throughout and juices run clear when pierced with fork, about 15-20 minutes. Transfer to warm plates, and garnish with mandarin oranges and a sprinkle of parsley.

SUGGESTED MENU

Sticky Fingers

Avocados with Kiwi Mint Salsa

Barbecue Voodoo

Mixed Greens with Honey Tarragon Vinaigrette

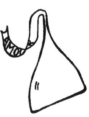

Playing With Fire

French Kisses

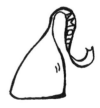

Hotsee Totsee

Grilled Asparagus

Wine

Chardonnay

♥ *Let's Do It*

…let's fall in love!

Chicken Kabobs with Lemon Basil Marinade

Step One:

½ cup olive oil
2 cloves garlic, minced
1 Tbsp. soy sauce
¼ cup chopped fresh basil
2 Tbsp. lemon juice
salt and pepper, to taste

Whisk all ingredients in bowl until blended.

Step Two:

2 boneless, skinless chicken breasts
1 small eggplant
red onions, quartered
½ lb. large brown mushrooms,
    sliced ½" thick
basil sprigs

Cut chicken and eggplant into bite-sized cubes and add to marinade. Add onions and mushrooms to marinade. Cover and marinate 30 minutes. Alternate chicken and vegetable cubes on skewers, and grill over medium heat, turning to brown evenly. Brush often with marinade. When chicken is white throughout and vegetables are tender, remove skewers to warm platter and garnish with basil sprigs.

SUGGESTED MENU

Sticky Fingers

Mediterranean Salsa

Barbecue Voodoo

Charred Red Pepper & White Bean Soup

Playing With Fire

♥*Let's Do It*

Hotsee Totsee

Grilled Polenta with Herbs

Wine

Sauvignon Blanc

♥*Chickalicious*

…you're lip smackin' good!

35 minutes

(marinate 1 hour)

Sweet Honey Mustard Chicken Breasts

Step One:

¼ tsp. dried oregano
¼ tsp. dried thyme
¼ tsp. black pepper
¼ tsp. cayenne
1 Tbsp. cider vinegar
¼ cup mustard
2 Tbsp. molasses
1 Tbsp. honey
1 Tbsp. vegetable oil

Combine seasonings in pan, add vinegar, and mix well. Put pan over medium heat and add remaining ingredients. Stirring constantly, bring mixture to a boil. Reduce heat and simmer 5 minutes, stirring occasionally.

Step Two:

2 boneless, skinless chicken breasts

Put chicken in shallow dish, pour sauce over evenly, and marinate in refrigerator 1 hour.

Step Three:

parsley, thyme, or oregano sprigs

Place chicken on oiled grill over medium heat. Grill, turning 2-3 times and brushing with sauce, until chicken is opaque throughout and juices run clear when pierced with fork, about 15-20 minutes. Transfer to warm plates and garnish with sprigs of herbs.

36

SUGGESTED MENU

Sticky Fingers

Artichoke and Red Pepper Spread

Barbecue Voodoo

Grilled Corn Salad

Playing With Fire

♥*Chickalicious*

Hotsee Totsee

Mediterranean Vegetables with Olive Pepper Relish

Wine

Chenin Blanc

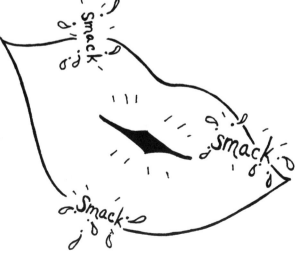

A Lick and a Promise

A promise is a debt unpaid, so let's settle up tonight!

(marinate 30 minutes)

Maple Barbecued Chicken

Step One:

½ cup maple syrup
1 Tbsp. tomato paste
1 Tbsp. wine vinegar
1½ Tbsp. chopped onion
¼ tsp. dry mustard
¼ tsp. pepper
salt, to taste

In large bowl, mix all ingredients together and blend well.

Step Two:

2 bone-in chicken breasts

Add chicken pieces to bowl and turn to coat. Cover and marinate for 30 minutes. Grill over medium-high heat for about 20 minutes, turning often, and brushing with marinade until cooked through.

SUGGESTED MENU

Sticky Fingers

Artichoke and Red Pepper Spread

Barbecue Voodoo

Grilled Corn Salad

Playing With Fire

A Lick and a Promise

Hotsee Totsee

Grilled Ratatouille

Wine

Chianti

I.O.U.
a might of
total indulgence.
me

Whole Lotta Hotta

Baby, is what you gotta lotta!

Hot Java Barbecued Chicken

Step One:

2 jalapeños

Halve, seed, and roast peppers over open flame or under broiler until charred. Transfer to paper bag, fold top tightly, and steam for 10 minutes. Scrape charred bits off peppers, chop, and remove to heavy saucepan.

Step Two:

³/₄ cup strong coffee
½ cup catsup
¼ cup tomato paste
¼ cup molasses
2 Tbsp. orange marmalade
2 Tbsp. cider vinegar
1½ Tbsp. Worcestershire sauce
2 tsp. Dijon mustard
dashes of Tabasco

Add all ingredients to sauce pan. Bring to a simmer over medium heat, stirring to blend. Cook over low heat until thickened, about 10-15 minutes. Remove from heat, and allow to cool.

Step Three:

1 chicken, cut up

Place chicken, skin side down on oiled grill over medium heat. Cook uncovered, 10-15 minutes, turning often, until well browned. Cover the grill; open vents half way and cook chicken 5 minutes. Brush chicken with sauce. Cover and cook 10-15 minutes more, brushing with sauce 2-3 more times. Chicken is done when opaque throughout and juices run clear.

SUGGESTED MENU

Sticky Fingers

Avocados with Kiwi Mint Salsa

Barbecue Voodoo

Mixed Greens with Honey Tarragon Vinaigrette

Playing With Fire

Whole Lotta Hotta

Hotsee Totsee

Two Potato Grill

Wine

Chianti

Saucy Aussie

How 'bout a little piece of heaven from Down Under?

Shrimp and Pineapple Skewers

Step One:

3 Tbsp. olive oil
2 Tbsp. lime juice
2 Tbsp. honey
2 Tbsp. chopped fresh parsley
1 Tbsp. finely minced ginger
1 Tbsp. grated lime zest
salt and pepper, to taste
¾ lb. large shrimp, peeled and deveined

Mix all ingredients except shrimp in medium bowl until well blended. Add shrimp and marinate 2 hours in refrigerator, stirring occasionally.

Step Two:

1 small pineapple, peeled and cored
lettuce leaves

Cut pineapple into bite-size chunks. Alternate shrimp and pineapple on skewers, and reserve remaining pineapple for another use. Cook over medium-high heat until shrimp are just firm and opaque. Serve on bed of lettuce leaves.

SUGGESTED MENU

Sticky Fingers

Avocados with Kiwi Mint Salsa

Barbecue Voodoo

Mixed Greens with Honey Tarragon Vinaigrette

Playing With Fire

♥ *Saucy Aussie*

Hotsee Totsee

Grilled Asparagus

Wine

Pinot Grigio

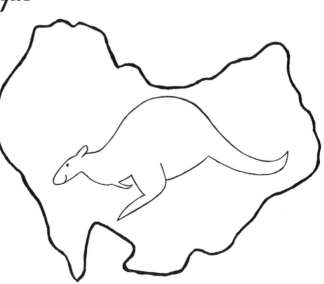

Bare Necessities

…will leave you wearing nothing but a smile!

Ahi in Orange Ginger Glaze

Step One:

¼ cup vegetable oil

3 Tbsp. soy sauce

2 Tbsp. dry sherry

1 Tbsp. frozen orange juice concentrate

1 Tbsp. minced orange zest

1½ tsp. minced fresh ginger

pepper, to taste

¾-1 lb. fresh ahi fillets, 1" thick

Whisk all ingredients except ahi in bowl until well blended. Put ahi in dish, pour marinade over and refrigerate for 2 hours, turning once.

Step Two:

Grill ahi over medium-high heat until it is still slightly translucent at center, about 4-5 minutes per side for medium. Do not over-cook.

SUGGESTED MENU

Sticky Fingers

Barbecued Pork Skewers

Barbecue Voodoo

Mixed Greens with Honey Tarragon Vinaigrette

Playing With Fire

Bare Necessities

Hotsee Totsee

Grilled Asparagus

Wine

Sauvignon Blanc

♥ Carte Blanche

Halibut a night of love…with no limits?

Grilled Halibut with Parsley Caper Mustard Sauce

Step One:

½ cup firmly packed parsley leaves
2 Tbsp. capers
1 Tbsp. Dijon mustard
1 clove garlic
¼ cup olive oil
1½ Tbsp. fresh lemon juice
salt and pepper, to taste

Combine all ingredients in food processor and process until finely minced.

Step Two:

1 lb. halibut, divided in two
olive oil, as needed
salt and pepper, to taste
parsley sprigs

Lightly brush halibut with oil, season with salt and pepper, and grill over medium heat about 2 minutes per side or until fish is opaque throughout. Remove to warm plates, nap with sauce, garnish with parsley sprigs, and serve.

SUGGESTED MENU

Sticky Fingers

Artichoke and Red Pepper Spread

Barbecue Voodoo

Charred Red Pepper & White Bean Soup

Playing With Fire

♥*Carte Blanche*

Hotsee Totsee

Grilled Ratatouille

Wine

Chardonnay

Spend it while
you can!

1475 28963 4137

BABYCAKES XOXO   KISSA

Hot Lips and Slow Sips

1 hour

…quick zips…bare hips…let's skinny dip!

Mahi Mahi with Macadamia Butter and Pineapple Relish

Step One:

½ pineapple, peeled and cored
1 small jalapeño
¼ cup minced fresh cilantro
½ orange, diced
½ lime, diced

For relish, cut pineapple lengthwise into 4-6 thick spears. Grill 2 spears over medium-high heat for 3-4 minutes per side. Remove from grill, dice, and put in bowl. Grill jalapeño until softened. Halve jalapeño, remove seeds and stem, and mince. Add jalapeño and remaining ingredients to bowl, blend well, and set aside.

Step Two:

2 oz. macadamia nuts, finely chopped
1 Tbsp. butter

Cook nuts in butter in small pan over low heat until browned, set aside.

Step Three:

pineapple spears
¾ lb. mahi mahi, 1" thick
1 lime, halved
salt, to taste

Grill remaining pineapple spears over medium-high heat until brown grill marks appear. Remove to plate. Sprinkle mahi mahi with lime juice and salt. Grill mahi mahi over medium heat until fish is just cooked through, about 4 minutes per side.

Step Four:

To serve, spoon pineapple relish onto warm plates and top with mahi mahi. Spoon a little macadamia nut butter on top. Lay grilled pineapple spears next to fish and serve extra pineapple relish on the side.

SUGGESTED MENU

Sticky Fingers

Barbecued Pork Skewers

Barbecue Voodoo

Mixed Greens with Honey Tarragon Vinaigrette

Playing With Fire

Hot Lips and Slow Sips

Hotsee Totsee

Grilled Asparagus

Wine

Chenin Blanc

♥ Night of the Iwanna

I wanna be loved bayou!

minutes

Shrimp and Sausage Skewers

Step One:
2 Tbsp. butter
1 clove garlic, minced
1 tsp. coarse-grained mustard
½ tsp. Worcestershire sauce
¼ tsp. horseradish
½ tsp. lemon juice
zest of ½ lemon
salt and pepper, to taste

For mustard butter, melt butter in small saucepan over medium heat, whisk in remaining ingredients, and set aside.

Step Two:
1 red onion, cut in small chunks
½ lb. polish sausage, cut in ½" slices
½ lb. shrimp, peeled and deveined
1 red bell pepper, cut in 1" pieces
1 green bell pepper, cut in 1" pieces

Divide onion wedges into 2-3 layers per piece. Alternate ingredients on skewers, pushing sausages on through skin side. Brush with mustard butter and grill over medium heat, 3 minutes per side. Serve mustard butter on side.

SUGGESTED MENU

Sticky Fingers

Mediterranean Salsa

Barbecue Voodoo

Grilled Tomato Basil Salad

Playing With Fire

♥*Night of the Iwanna*

Hotsee Totsee

Two Potato Grill

Wine

Pinot Grigio

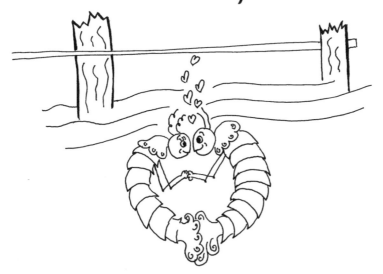

Thief of Hearts

Steal her heart away with this entrée!

Salmon Fillet with Cucumber Dill Sauce

Step One:

½ cup plain yogurt
¼ cup low-fat mayonnaise
¼ cup seeded, peeled, and chopped
    cucumber
2 Tbsp. chopped fresh dill
2 tsp. fresh lemon juice
1 tsp. lemon zest
salt and pepper, to taste

Combine all ingredients in bowl, stirring to blend. Refrigerate for 1 hour.

Step Two:

¾ lb. salmon fillet, 1" thick
oil, as needed
salt and pepper, to taste
lemon or cucumber slices
dill sprigs

Cut salmon into 2 pieces. Brush skinless side lightly with oil and season. Place skin side down on oiled grill, cover, and cook over medium heat until bottom edges begin to turn opaque, about 5 minutes. Turn salmon, continue to cook until outside is opaque but center is still translucent, about 2-4 minutes. Transfer salmon to warm plates, garnish with cucumber/lemon slices and dill, and serve with sauce.

SUGGESTED MENU

Sticky Fingers

Artichoke and Red Pepper Spread

Barbecue Voodoo

Grilled Corn Salad

Playing With Fire

Thief of Hearts

Hotsee Totsee

Grilled Asparagus

Wine

Chardonnay

Tempting Ewe

...is what I like to do best!

Lamb Chops in Herbed Béarnaise Sauce

Step One:

1½ Tbsp. minced shallots
½ clove garlic, minced
2 Tbsp. fresh lemon juice
¼ cup dry white wine
½ Tbsp. tarragon
½ Tbsp. chervil
salt and pepper, to taste

To make béarnaise sauce, combine all ingredients in small saucepan and boil over medium-high heat until about 2 tablespoons remain, forming a glaze.

Step Two:

3 large egg yolks
⅛ tsp. cayenne
½ cup butter, melted

Put egg yolks and cayenne in blender. Blend on high 10-15 seconds. Add glaze and, with machine running on high speed, butter in slow steady stream. Run on high 1 minute, off 30 seconds. Repeat until sauce is thickened. Put blender jar in pan of warm water while grilling chops.

Step Three:

¾ -1 lb. lamb tenderloin chops,
    1-1½" thick
olive oil, as needed
salt and pepper, to taste
2 Tbsp. snipped chives

Trim lamb chops, brush lightly with oil, and season with salt and pepper. Grill, turning 2-3 times, until browned but still pink in the center, about 8 minutes. Remove to warmed plates, spoon a little béarnaise over chops, sprinkle with chives, and serve.

SUGGESTED MENU

Sticky Fingers

Sun-dried Tomato Olive Toasts

Barbecue Voodoo

*Mixed Greens with Honey
Tarragon Vinaigrette*

Playing With Fire

Tempting Ewe

Hotsee Totsee

*Mediterranean Vegetables
with Olive Pepper Relish*

Wine

Zinfandel

Live 8 p.m.

A night of Romance

I'm All Yours!

whatever makes you happy

Lovin' U 2-Nite

Light My Fire

...and I'll do the same for ewe!

Lamb Kabobs with Lemon Garlic Marinade

Step One:

½ cup olive oil

2 Tbsp. fresh lemon juice

3 cloves garlic, crushed

1 Tbsp. dry white wine

1 bay leaf

½ tsp. dried oregano

½ tsp. dried rosemary

salt and pepper, to taste

In medium bowl, whisk all ingredients until well blended.

Step Two:

1¼ lbs. lean boneless lamb, cut into 1½" cubes

Pour marinade over lamb, cover, and refrigerate overnight.

Step Three:

1 large red onion, cut in wedges

½ lb. mushroom caps, cleaned

4 Roma tomatoes, quartered

1 green bell pepper, seeded and cut into 1" chunks

Divide onion wedges into 2-3 layers per piece. Alternate lamb and vegetables on skewers. Baste with marinade and grill over medium heat, turning often, until done, about 7-8 minutes.

SUGGESTED MENU

Sticky Fingers

Mediterranean Salsa

Barbecue Voodoo

Mixed Greens with Honey Tarragon Vinaigrette

Playing With Fire

♥*Light My Fire*

Hotsee Totsee

Mediterranean Vegetables with Olive Pepper Relish

Wine

Sangiovese

♥Déjà Blue

Let's do that all over again!

Blue Cheese Lamb Burgers with Sautéed Spinach

Step One:

2 Tbsp. dried cranberries
1 oz. blue cheese
1 oz. cream cheese
2 Tbsp. snipped chives

Put cranberries in cup of hot water, set aside.
Put cheeses and chives in small bowl and blend
well. Divide into two patties.

Step Two:

1 lb. ground lamb
2 Tbsp. finely chopped onion
salt and pepper, to taste

In bowl, combine lamb and onion, season
liberally, and form into 4 flattened patties. Put
each cheese patty between two lamb patties
and press edges to seal.

Step Three:

¼ cup chopped onion
1 clove garlic, minced
½ cup sliced mushrooms
1 Tbsp. olive oil
1 bunch spinach, washed and
    stems removed

In large frying pan over medium heat, sauté
onion, garlic, and mushrooms in oil until
golden. Add spinach and continue cooking
until wilted. Drain cranberries and stir into
spinach. Cover and remove from heat.

Step Four:

Grill lamb patties over medium heat 7-8
minutes per side until done. Divide spinach
onto warm plates, top with lamb patties, and
serve.

Sticky Fingers

Artichoke and Red Pepper Spread

Barbecue Voodoo

Mixed Greens with Honey Tarragon Vinaigrette

Playing With Fire

Déjà Blue

Hotsee Totsee

Grilled Asparagus

Wine

Sirah

♥ Carpe P.M.

Let's seize the night!

Penne Pasta with Summer Vegetables and Feta

Step One:

1 red bell pepper
1 yellow bell pepper

Halve, seed, and roast peppers over open flame or under broiler until charred. Transfer to paper bag, fold top tightly, and steam for 10 minutes. Scrape charred bits off peppers, cut into bite-size chunks, and remove to bowl.

Step Two:

1 zucchini, sliced lengthwise ¼" thick
1 pattypan squash, sliced ¼" thick
oil, as needed
salt and pepper, to taste
4 tomatoes, cored

Brush squashes with oil and season. Grill over medium heat until tender, about 10 minutes. Remove to cutting board and cut into bite-size chunks. Grill tomatoes until skin loosens, remove to cutting board, dice, and remove to bowl.

Step Three:

2 cloves garlic, minced
1 tsp. olive oil
½ lb. penne pasta, cooked according
   to package directions
8 basil leaves, sliced in ribbons
salt and pepper, to taste
¼ cup herbed croutons
⅓ cup crumbled feta

In saucepan, sauté garlic in oil until tender; add tomatoes and their juices. Simmer on medium heat, 5 minutes. Add penne, grilled vegetables, basil, salt, and pepper, and heat through. Serve in big bowls sprinkled with croutons and feta.

Sticky Fingers

Mediterranean Salsa

Barbecue Voodoo

Mixed Greens with Honey Tarragon Vinaigrette

Playing With Fire

♥*Carpe P.M.*

Hotsee Totsee

Mediterranean Vegetables with Olive Pepper Relish

Wine

Sauvignon Blanc

Bikini Fettucini

Strings or thongs, you're singin' my song!

Caramelized Onion and Pepper Pasta

Step One:

2 red bell peppers

Halve, seed, and roast peppers over open flame or under broiler until charred. Transfer to paper bag, fold top tightly, and steam for 10 minutes. Scrape charred bits off peppers, cut into ¼" strips, and set aside.

Step Two:

¼ cup olive oil
1 Spanish onion, halved and thinly sliced
1 clove garlic, crushed
salt and pepper, to taste

Heat oil in large frying pan over low heat and stir in onion. Sauté until soft and golden, about 6-7 minutes. Stir in peppers and garlic, sauté 1 minute, then add salt and pepper.

Step Three:

8 oz. fettucini
¼ cup pine nuts
¼ cup chopped fresh parsley

Cook fettucini according to package directions until al dente, or just tender to bite. Meanwhile, toast nuts in dry pan over low-medium heat until golden. In large serving bowl, toss pasta lightly with sauce, sprinkle with pine nuts and parsley, and serve.

SUGGESTED MENU

Sticky Fingers

Artichoke and Red Pepper Spread

Barbecue Voodoo

Grilled Tomato Basil Salad

Playing With Fire

Bikini Fettucini

Hotsee Totsee

Grilled Polenta with Herbs

Wine

Chardonnay

Viva Roma

It's la dolce vita, dining al fresco with you!

Grilled Vegetable Pizza with Bruschetta and Pesto

Step One:
⅓ cup finely chopped shallots
2 cloves garlic, minced
1 Tbsp. light olive oil
8 Roma tomatoes, finely chopped
1 Tbsp. finely chopped fresh basil,
    or 1 tsp. dried

For bruschetta, sauté shallots and garlic in oil over medium heat until soft and lightly browned. Add tomatoes, mashing with wooden spoon. Add basil and cook until reduced and only a little liquid remains, about 15-20 minutes.

Step Two:
⅓ cup chopped fresh basil
⅓ cup chopped fresh parsley
⅓ cup freshly grated Parmesan
⅓ cup walnuts
1 clove garlic
¼ cup light olive oil

For pesto, put all ingredients except oil in processor and pulse until mixed. With machine running, add oil in slow stream until just blended.

Step Three:
½ eggplant, cut in ½" slices
1 zucchini, cut in ½" diagonal slices
1 crookneck squash, cut in ½" slices
1 red bell pepper, cut in ½" rings
8-10 mushrooms, cut in ¼" slices

Grill vegetables on oiled grill screen or grill over medium-high heat until just tender.

Step Four:
1 large pre-baked pizza crust
1½ cup grated mozzarella

Preheat oven to 400°. Spread bruschetta over pizza crust. Spread pesto over brushcetta. Sprinkle with one third of mozzarella. Dice eggplant and spread on pizza, followed by zucchini, and another third of mozzarella. Layer on squash and mushrooms. Chop peppers and sprinkle on top. Sprinkle with remaining mozzarella and bake 10 minutes. Optional: grill a boneless, skinless chicken breast, brushed with oil and balsamic vinegar. Slice thinly, and add to squash and mushroom layer.

SUGGESTED MENU

Sticky Fingers

Sun-dried Tomato Olive Toasts

Barbecue Voodoo

Charred Red Pepper & White Bean Soup

Playing With Fire

Viva Roma

Wine

Vioqnier

Wizard of Aaahs

Let my spicy sauce cast its spell on you!

Pork Chops in Smokey Bacon Barbecue Sauce

Step One:

2-3 pork chops, 1" thick
1 onion, thinly sliced
2 cloves garlic, minced
2 Tbsp. hot pepper sauce

Put pork chops in shallow dish. Combine remaining ingredients and pour over chops. Cover and set aside for 2 hours at room temperature.

Step Two:

1 clove garlic
1 small red bell pepper, seeded and
    quartered
½ jalapeño, seeded
¼ cup firmly packed parsley

Put all ingredients in food processor and mince.

Step Three:

3 slices bacon, cut in ½" pieces
1 small onion, coarsely chopped
2 medium tomatoes, chopped
⅔ cup dark beer
¼ cup catsup
2 Tbsp. molasses
1 Tbsp. tomato paste
½ tsp. Worcestershire sauce
¼ tsp. hot pepper sauce
½ tsp. each chili powder, salt, ground
    ginger, dry mustard
¼ tsp. each dried basil, oregano, cumin
$\frac{1}{8}$ tsp. cayenne
$1\frac{1}{2}$ tsp. bourbon

Sauté bacon in frying pan over medium heat until it gives up all its fat. Discard all but 1 tablespoon of fat. Add onion and sauté until golden, about 5-7 minutes. Add mixture from step 2 and sauté until tender, about 3 minutes. Add remaining ingredients except bourbon and simmer 30 minutes. Stir bourbon into sauce and turn heat to low.

Step Four:

Remove pork chops from marinade and pat dry with paper towels. Grill chops over medium heat, turning once, until evenly browned, about 8 minutes. Brush often with barbecue sauce. Spoon sauce onto warmed plates, top with chops, spoon a little more sauce over chops, and serve.

SUGGESTED MENU

Sticky Fingers
Avocados with Kiwi Mint Salsa

Barbecue Voodoo
Grilled Corn Salad

Playing With Fire
Wizard of Aaahs

Hotsee Totsee
Two Potato Grill

Wine
Chianti

Ribbing On Love

…and loving it!

Baby Back Ribs in Honey Ginger Sauce

Step One:

1 tsp. celery seed
1 carrot, chopped
½ onion, cut into rings
1 side pork spareribs

Fill large pot ⅔ full with water. Add celery seed, carrot, and onion. Bring to a boil and add ribs. Turn flame to medium low and simmer 1 hour.

Step Two:

2 cups chicken broth
1 cup soy sauce
¾ cup catsup
½ cup sherry
½ cup Çuracao (or other orange liqueur)
½ cup honey
½ tsp. minced fresh ginger
2 large cloves garlic, minced

Combine all ingredients. Pour into large baking dish. Add ribs and marinate in refrigerator for 24 hours.

Step Three:

⅔ cup honey
2 Tbsp. soy sauce
1 tsp. dried ground ginger
¼ cup reserved marinade

To make glaze: combine all ingredients in small bowl. If baking, preheat oven to 375°. Place ribs on baking sheet, brush with glaze, and bake 20-30 minutes. If grilling, brush ribs with glaze and grill over medium heat, about 10 minutes per side. Reposition on grill often to avoid uneven browning.

SUGGESTED MENU

Sticky Fingers

Avocados with Kiwi Mint Salsa

Barbecue Voodoo

Grilled Corn Salad

Playing With Fire

Ribbing on Love

Hotsee Totsee

Grilled Asparagus

Wine

Sauvignon Blanc

♥ Naked Truth

...a clothing optional entrée!

Apricot Dijon Pork Chops

Step One:

½ cup apricot jam
2 Tbsp. Dijon mustard
2 Tbsp. soy sauce

Combine all ingredients in small pan and cook over medium heat until jam melts, stirring often.

Step Two:

salt and pepper, to taste
2 pork loin chops, ¾" thick

Season pork chops and grill over medium heat, 5-6 minutes. Turn and brush with sauce. Continue to grill about 5-6 more minutes, until done or no longer pink in middle. Reheat remaining sauce and serve with chops.

Sticky Fingers

Sun-dried Tomato Olive Toasts

Barbecue Voodoo

Mixed Greens with Honey Tarragon Vinaigrette

Playing With Fire

♥*Naked Truth*

Hotsee Totsee

Two Potato Grill

Wine

Pinot Noir

Dare To Be Bare

…and you'll be tickled pink!

Fresh Crab and Grilled Asparagus Salad

Step One:
⅓ cup light olive oil
3 Tbsp. fresh lemon juice
2 Tbsp. chopped fresh parsley
1 tsp. dried basil
1 tsp. dried chervil
salt and fresh ground pepper, to taste
10-12 spears fresh asparagus, trimmed

For vinaigrette, whisk all ingredients except asparagus in small bowl until well blended. Pour ¼ cup of vinaigrette into second bowl. Put asparagus into glass dish, pour remaining vinaigrette over asparagus, and refrigerate for 30 minutes.

Step Two:
1½ Tbsp. minced shallots or green
    onions
1 clove garlic, minced
salt and pepper, to taste
½ lb. fresh crabmeat

Add shallots, garlic, and seasonings to bowl with reserved vinaigrette and blend well. Put crabmeat in medium bowl. Add enough vinaigrette to moisten crab, about 2 table-spoons, toss gently, and set aside.

Step Three:
mixed salad greens (e.g., romaine,
    radicchio, frisee)
2 Tbsp. freshly grated Parmesan
1 Tbsp. chopped fresh parsley

Tear greens into bite-size pieces and divide onto two dinner plates. Remove asparagus from vinaigrette. Grill asparagus over medium heat until tender. Fan asparagus spears onto greens and top with a mound of crab. Drizzle with the remaining vinaigrette, and sprinkle with fresh Parmesan and chopped parsley. Serve with warm crusty French bread.

SUGGESTED MENU

Sticky Fingers

Sun-Dried Tomato Olive Toasts

Barbecue Voodoo

*Charred Red Pepper &
White Bean Soup*

Playing With Fire

♥Dare To Be Bare

Hotsee Totsee

Grilled Polenta with Herbs

Wine

Sauvignon Blanc

♥Double Dipping

Twice is nice!

Curried Papaya and Grilled Salmon Salad

Step One:
2 Tbsp. vegetable oil
1 Tbsp. canned light, unsweetened
   coconut milk
1 Tbsp. Thai green curry paste
2 tsp. soy sauce
1 tsp. sesame oil
1 tsp. minced garlic
1 tsp. finely grated fresh ginger
¾ lb. salmon fillet, cut in half

For marinade, whisk first seven ingredients together in a medium bowl until well blended. Pour half of marinade into shallow dish, add salmon, and spoon remaining marinade over salmon. Cover; marinate 1 hour at room temperature.

Step Two:
¼ cup light olive oil
2 Tbsp. fresh lemon juice
1½ tsp. soy sauce
½ tsp. salt

For dressing, whisk all ingredients in bowl until emulsified. Set aside.

Step Three:

Remove salmon from marinade and drain on rack for 10 minutes. Turn and drain additional 10 minutes. Grill salmon over medium-high heat 3-4 minutes. Turn and grill 2-3 minutes longer or until it flakes easily with fork.

Step Four:
1 lb. mixed salad greens (e.g., romaine,
   red leaf, butter leaf, frisee)
1 cup bean sprouts
½ papaya, seeded, peeled, and diced
½ cup macadamia nuts, coarsely
   chopped

Meanwhile, combine greens and sprouts in large bowl and toss lightly with lemon dressing. Divide onto two dinner plates and sprinkle with papaya. Top with salmon and sprinkle with macadamia nuts.

SUGGESTED MENU

Sticky Fingers

Barbecued Pork Skewers

Barbecue Voodoo

*Charred Red Pepper &
White Bean Soup*

Playing With Fire

♥Double Dipping

Wine

Chenin Blanc

Hot Moves

No matter where I go, you're where I belong!

1 hour, 10 minutes

(marinate 20 minutes)

Marinated Salad with Grilled Portabella Mushrooms

Step One:

1 clove garlic, split
¼ cup olive oil
4 Tbsp. balsamic vinegar
salt and pepper, to taste

For dressing, put garlic in oil and allow to stand 15–20 minutes. Whisk oil, vinegar, salt, and pepper until well blended.

Step Two:

1 red bell pepper, halved and seeded

Roast pepper over flame or under broiler until charred. Place in paper bag, fold top tightly, and steam 10 minutes. Remove pepper from bag, scrape off charred bits, cut into thin strips, and put in large bowl. Set aside.

Step Three:

2 ears sweet corn, blanched and
    kernels removed
1 cup halved cherry or grape tomatoes
12 niçoise olives, pitted and chopped
¼ cup sun-dried tomatoes in oil,
    drained and julienned
¼ cup basil leaves, cut in thin strips
¼ cup red onions, chopped
1 cup herbed croutons

Remove garlic from dressing. Add all ingredients to bowl with pepper and toss with dressing. Allow ingredients to marinate 20 minutes, stirring occasionally.

Step Four:

¼ cup pine nuts
mixed salad greens (e.g., romaine,
    arugula, spinach)
2 portabella mushrooms, cut in 1" slices
2 Tbsp. freshly grated Asiago cheese

Toast pine nuts in dry frying pan over low heat until golden, about 5 minutes. Tear greens into bite-size pieces and divide onto two dinner plates. Spoon corn and tomato mixture on top of greens. Brush mushroom slices with dressing and grill over medium heat until tender. Remove from grill, fan mushroom slices on top of salad, and sprinkle with pine nuts and Asiago.

SUGGESTED MENU

Sticky Fingers

Sun-dried Tomato Olive Toasts

Barbecue Voodoo

Charred Red Pepper & White Bean Soup

Playing With Fire

Hot Moves

Hotsee Totsee

Grilled Polenta with Herbs

Wine

Sauvignon Blanc

Grilled Asparagus

20 minutes

Step One:

1 lb. asparagus, trimmed
1 Tbsp. olive oil
2 Tbsp. freshly grated Parmesan
2 tsp. fresh lemon zest

Brush asparagus with oil and grill on rack over medium heat, turning often, until browned, about 10 minutes. Remove to warm platter, sprinkle with Parmesan and lemon zest, and serve.

Mediterranean Vegetables with Olive Pepper Relish

45 minutes

Step One:

2 red bell peppers
1 16-oz. can black olives, sliced
1 Tbsp. olive oil
2 heaping Tbsp. chopped sun-dried
    tomatoes, in oil
1 Tbsp. lemon juice
1 large clove garlic, crushed

Halve, seed, and roast peppers over open flame or under broiler until charred. Transfer to paper bag, fold top tightly, and steam for 10 minutes. Scrape charred bits off peppers, chop, and put in bowl. Add olives. In separate bowl, whisk together remaining ingredients and stir into peppers and olives. Set aside.

Step Two:

2 Tbsp. light olive oil
1 clove garlic, minced
salt and pepper, to taste
½ eggplant
1 medium zucchini
1 summer squash
10 large brown mushrooms
¼ cup chopped fresh cilantro

Mix oil, garlic, salt, and pepper in plastic bag. Cut vegetables into bite-size pieces, put into bag, and toss until coated. Thread onto skewers or grill on oiled grill screen over medium heat, 10-12 minutes, turning often, until done. Turn vegetables into bowl, toss with relish, stir in cilantro, and serve.

Two Potato Grill

45 minutes

Step One:
1 large baking potato
1 large sweet potato
1–2 Tbsp. oil
⅛ tsp. garlic salt
salt and pepper, to taste

Peel and slice potatoes 1" thick. Put oil and seasonings in bowl; add potatoes and toss to coat lightly. Grill potatoes directly on rack over medium heat, covered, for 10-15 minutes, moving often to prevent burning. Turn potatoes, cook 10 minutes more, brush with herb butter, turn again, and continue until tender.

Step Two:
2 Tbsp. butter
½ tsp. dried sage
½ tsp. dried thyme

Meanwhile melt butter in small bowl and add herbs. Brush on cooking potatoes, as needed. Serve.

Grilled Ratatouille

30 minutes

Step One:
½ eggplant, sliced in 1" pieces
1 zucchini, sliced lengthwise
1 red bell pepper, halved and seeded
1 yellow bell pepper, halved and seeded
1 red onion, sliced in 1" rings
olive oil, as needed
salt and pepper, to taste

Brush vegetables with olive oil and sprinkle with seasonings. Grill over medium heat, turning often, until tender, about 10-12 minutes. Remove to cutting board, dice vegetables, and put in bowl.

Step Two:
1 tomato, chopped
1 Tbsp. light olive oil
salt and pepper, to taste
1 Tbsp. minced fresh herbs (e.g., basil, thyme, parsley)

Add tomato and olive oil to bowl, toss to coat. Sprinkle vegetables with seasonings and herbs, toss lightly, and serve.

Grilled Polenta with Herbs

(marinate 1-2 hours)

Step One:

1 cup water
2 cups low-salt chicken broth
1 cup polenta
1 Tbsp. minced fresh rosemary
¼ cup butter
⅓ cup freshly grated Parmesan

In deep saucepan, bring water and broth to a boil over high heat. Turn heat to medium; slowly add polenta, stirring constantly with wood spoon, until it pulls away from pan, about 20 minutes. Remove from heat and stir in remaining ingredients. Spoon polenta into square cake pan, pressing to even it out. Cover and refrigerate 1-2 hours.

Step Two:

olive oil, as needed
rosemary sprigs
cherry tomatoes, halved

Dip pan into hot water to loosen polenta. Run knife around edges and invert onto cutting board. Cut into squares or shapes, brush with oil and grill over medium heat until browned and crisp. Generously sprinkle with Parmesan, and garnish with rosemary and tomatoes.

SUBJECT INDEX

Lamb

RECIPE INDEX

Mmm, Mmm, GOOD
(Notes)

Mmm, Mmm, GOOD
(Notes)